Learning Short-take

EFFECTIVE TIME MANAGEMENT

Clear the clutter and focus on what's important

CATHERINE MATTISKE

TPC - The Performance Company Pty Ltd
Level 20, Darling Park
Tower 2, 201 Sussex Street,
Sydney NSW 2000
Australia

ACN 077 455 273
email: tpc@tpc.net.au
Website: www.catherinemattiske.com

© TPC – The Performance Company Pty Limited
First edition published in 2006
Second edition published in 2011
Third edition published in 2022

All rights reserved. Apart from any fair dealing for the purposes of study, research or review, as permitted under Australian copyright law, no part of this publication may be reproduced by any means without the written permission of the copyright owner. Every effort has been made to obtain permission relating to information reproduced in this publication.

The information in this publication is based on the current state of commercial and industry practice, applicable legislation, general law and the general circumstances as at the date of publication. No person shall rely on any of the contents of this publication and the publisher and the author expressly exclude all liability for direct and indirect loss suffered by any person resulting in any way from the use of or reliance on this publication or any part of it. Any options and advice are offered solely in pursuance of the author's and the publisher's intention to provide information, and have not been specifically sought.

For eBook version: By payment of the required fees, you have been granted the non-exclusive, non-transferable right to access and read the text of this e-book on screen. No part of this text may be reproduced, transmitted, downloaded, decompiled, reverse engineered, or stored in or introduced into any information storage retrieval system, in any form or by any means, whether the electronic or mechanical, now known or hereinafter invented, without the express permission of the author.

 A catalogue record for this book is available from the National Library of Australia

National Library of Australia
Cataloguing-in-Publication data

Mattiske, Catherine
Effective Time Management: Clear the clutter and focus on what's important

ISBN 978-1-921547-09-6

1. Occupational training 2. Learning I. Title

370.113

Distributed by TPC - The Performance Company - www.catherinemattiske.com
For further information contact TPC - The Performance Company, Sydney Australia on +61 (02) 9555 1953.

HELLO.

Welcome to the Learning Short-take® process!

This Learning Short-take® is a bite sized learning package that aims to improve your skills and provide you with an opportunity for personal and professional development to achieve success in your role.

This Learning Short-take® combines self study with workplace activities in a unique learning system to keep you motivated and energized.
So let's get started!

Step 1:
What's inside?

- Learning Short-take®. This section contains all of the learning content and will guide you through the learning process.
- Learning Activities. You will be prompted to complete these as you read through.
- Learning Journal. This is a summary of your key learnings.
  Update it when prompted.
- Skill Development Action Plan. Learning is about taking action. This is your action plan where you'll plan how you will implement your learning.

Step 2:
Complete the Learning Short-take®

- Learning Short-takes® are best completed in a quiet environment that is free of distractions.
- Schedule time in your calendar to complete the Learning Short-take® and prioritize this time as an investment in your own professional development.
- Depending on the title, most participants complete the Learning Short-take® from 90 minutes to 2.5 hours.

Step 3:
Meet with your Manager/Coach

- Schedule a 30 minute meeting with your Manager or Coach.
- At this meeting share your completed Activities, Learning Journal and Skill Development Action Plan.
- Most importantly, discuss and agree on how you will implement your learning in your role.

GET VIP ACCESS TO YOUR MATERIALS

This Learning Short-take® includes an interactive activity book, associated tools and job aids, plus a bonus eBook.

1 Visit
https://www.catherinemattiske.com/books

2 Select your book

3 Click: **VIP ACCESS**

4 Enter the code: **ETM2022152**

WELCOME

Effective Time Management
Clear the Clutter and Focus on What's Important

Effective Time Management combines self-study with realistic workplace activities to provide the key skills and techniques that allow you to manage your time more effectively. You will learn to do the things you 'have to do' more efficiently, and generate more time for the things you 'want to do'. You will learn tips, tricks and techniques to ensure a positive return on your investment in time, increasing success in both your work and personal life.

Time is our most unique and valuable resource. We all have 24 hours in a day, 168 hours in a week, and we spend it at the same rate. Time management is about more than time - it is really about managing our lives. **Effective Time Management** will assist you to balance priorities, achieve more, be more efficient and learn to maximize minutes!

Effective Time Management includes the **Daily To Do List** and the **Weekly Planner**, provided to you as free downloadable tools.

Now let's get started!

1	Learning Short-take® > Start here
2	Learning Journal 53
3	Skill Development Action Plan 59
4	Quick Reference 65
5	Next Steps 79

> *"Time is what prevents everything from happening at once."*
>
> JOHN ARCHIBALD WHEELER

"

*Time is an equal opportunity employer. Each human being has exactly the same number of hours and minutes every day.
Rich people can't buy more hours. Scientists can't invent new minutes.
And you can't save time to spend it on another day. Even so, time is amazingly fair and forgiving. No matter how much time you've wasted in the past, you still have an entire tomorrow.*

DENIS WAITELY

Section 1

LEARNING SHORT-TAKE®

WHAT'S IN THIS LEARNING SHORT-TAKE®

"Time is a dressmaker specializing in alterations."

FAITH BALDWIN

Table of Contents

How to Complete Your Learning Short-take®	5
Activity Checklist	6
Learning Objectives	7
Let's Get Started	8
Part 1 - Getting Started	9
Imagine…	10
Goal Setting	14
Part 2 - Time Matrix	19
The Time Matrix	20
Part 3 - Daily and Weekly Actions	25
Planning & Prioritizing	26
The Daily To Do List	29
The Weekly Planner	32
Part 4 - Tips and Traps	37
Managing Unplanned Tasks & Interruptions	38
Clearing the Clutter	42
Time Management Quick Tips	44
Part 5 - A Final Thought	49
One Grain at a Time…	50

HOW TO COMPLETE YOUR LEARNING SHORT-TAKE®

1. **Reflect on your current skills and abilities** in managing your time and how this impacts on your effectiveness at work.

2. **Complete the Initial Skills Self-Assessment.**

3. Highlight specific skill areas that you believe you could develop more. Add these to the **Learning Journal.** Add to your Learning Journal as you go.

4. When you have completed this Learning Short-take® **meet with your Manager/Coach.** In this meeting, you will jointly establish a personal **Skill Development Action Plan.**

5. **Subject to your coach's final review** and assessment, you will either sign off the module, or undertake further skill development as appropriate.

"Time is what we want most, but... what we use worst."

WILLAIM PENN

ACTIVITY CHECKLIST

During this Learning Short-take® you will be prompted to complete the following activities:

- Activity # 1 - Initial Skills Self-Assessment   11
- Activity # 2 - Top Ten Time Robbers   13
- Activity # 3 - Goal Setting   17
- Activity # 4 - The Time Matrix   22
- Activity # 5 - My Biological Prime Time   28
- Activity # 6 - The Daily To Do List   31
- Activity # 7 - The Weekly Planner   35
- Activity # 8 - Managing Interruptions   40
- Activity # 9 - Time Management Quick Tips   47
- Learning Journal   53
- Skill Development Action Plan   59

"Time is the longest distance between two places."

TENNESSEE WILLIAMS

LEARNING OBJECTIVES

After you have completed this Learning Short-take®, you should be able to:

- Identify your own habits and time management behavior.
- Set short, medium and long term goals.
- Weed out tasks that are unimportant or a waste of time.
- Prioritize your work and create daily and weekly planners.
- Make instant changes to your workspace.
- Handle interruptions and avoid sidetracks.

"For fast acting relief, try slowing down."

LILY TOMLIN

LET'S GET STARTED

"Lost, yesterday, somewhere between sunrise and sunset, two golden hours, each set with 60 diamond minutes; no reward is offered for they are gone forever."

HORACE MANN

Time is our most unique and valuable resource. It is the one thing that we all have in common: we all have 24 hours in a day and 168 hours in a week. We cannot slow time down, stop time, or negotiate with time. Time is irretrievable and once wasted it is gone forever. Control and discipline are required to make the most of every minute.

However, effective time management is about more than just time. It is really about managing our lives, and controlling the events in our lives to increase productivity and create more time for personal and professional endeavours. It is about conditioning the environment, rather than allowing the environment to condition us. Effective time management can only be achieved through improved planning, prioritizing, and delegating; then identifying what we can change about our habits, routines and attitude to protect planned time. Time can be our biggest asset if we know how to manage it properly. If we can find ways to boost productivity, we can accomplish more in our day, impress customers and employers and leave ourselves more free time to enjoy life. It's that simple.

GETTING STARTED

PART 1

IMAGINE...

There is a bank that credits your account each morning with $86,400. It carries over no balance from day to day. Every evening it deletes whatever part of the balance you failed to use during the day. What would you do? Draw out ALL OF IT, of course!!!

Each of us has such a bank. Its name is TIME. Every morning, it credits you with 86,400 seconds. Every night it writes off, as lost, whatever of this you failed to invest to good purpose. It carries over no balance. It allows no overdraft.

Each day it opens a new account for you. Each night it burns the remains of the day. If you fail to use the day's deposits, the loss is yours.

There is no going back. There is no drawing against the "tomorrow". You must live in the present on today's deposits. Invest it so as to get from it the utmost in health, happiness, and success! The clock is running. Make the most of today.

Complete Activity # 1
Initial Skills Self-Assessment

Complete Activity # 2
Top Ten Time Robbers

ACTIVITY 1: INITIAL SKILLS SELF-ASSESSMENT

Understanding how you currently manage your time and knowing how to improve time management effectiveness is critical to job success. This assessment covers the key skills required to control your time in order to improve work performance.

Rate yourself on each of the techniques.
7 is competent and confident, little need for improvement
4 is average, needs improvement
1 is uncomfortable, major need for improvement

- Note specific areas of improvement related to each that you would like to develop. Be sure to include your reasons for your rating in each skill, as this reasoning will be a key part of the initial goal setting session with your coach.
- Start thinking about a personal development plan and identify two or three things you could do to improve your skills in this area and write them in the space provided.

I...	Rating	Reasoning
arrive on time and am prepared for meetings	1 2 3 4 5 6 7	
read my emails and messages on the day which I receive them	1 2 3 4 5 6 7	
am able to complete tasks without interruptions from colleagues	1 2 3 4 5 6 7	
decide how many time a day I can be interrupted	1 2 3 4 5 6 7	
reserve certain hours for visits from colleagues	1 2 3 4 5 6 7	
limit the duration of my phone or virtual calls	1 2 3 4 5 6 7	
decide how many phone/virtual calls I can deal with personally in a day	1 2 3 4 5 6 7	

ACTIVITY 1: CONTINUED

I...	Rating	Reasoning
keep the contents of my in-tray and inbox to a manageable size	1 2 3 4 5 6 7	
clear my desk of all paperwork	1 2 3 4 5 6 7	
perform housekeeping checks on my computer files and paper files	1 2 3 4 5 6 7	
delegate tasks to colleagues where appropriate	1 2 3 4 5 6 7	
follow up on the work that I have delegated	1 2 3 4 5 6 7	
achieve the tight balance between thinking time and action time	1 2 3 4 5 6 7	
make a list of the things that I need to do each day	1 2 3 4 5 6 7	
prioritize tasks according to what is important	1 2 3 4 5 6 7	
distinguish between 'urgent' and 'important' tasks	1 2 3 4 5 6 7	
keep work to a certain number of hours everyday – and no more	1 2 3 4 5 6 7	

Personal development plan ideas:

1

2

Now update your Learning Journal (page 53)

© 2022, TPC - The Performance Company Pty Limited. All rights reserved.

ACTIVITY 2: TOP TEN TIME ROBBERS

Circle the time robbers that you feel steal the most time from you.

For your top 3 time robbers think of some strategies that you could implement to miminize their impact on your time. Come back and add to these strategies after you have completed the Learning Short-take®.

Time Robber	Strategies to miminize impact on my time
1.	
2.	
3.	

Now update your Learning Journal (page 53)

GOAL SETTING

> *"The reason most people never reach their goals is that they don't define them, or ever seriously consider them as believable or achievable."*
>
> DENIS WATLEY

From a time management perspective, your life is a sequence of big and small choices determined by your goals. It is those choices that you really manage, not the flow of time. Goals give your life and the way you spend your time, direction. They help guide your conscious and subconscious decisions towards success, helping you to realize both personal and professional achievements.

The first step in effectively managing time is to develop an explicit statement of long-term goals. Your optimum goals are those which cause you to "stretch" but not "break" as you strive for success. Goals should be SMART (Specific, Measurable, Attainable, Realistic, and Tangible).

S pecific — Your goal must be specific.

M easurable — You must be able to measure progress towards your goal.

A ttainable — Your goal must be something that you can actually attain.

R ealistic — Your goal must be realistic, given who you are.

T angible — Your goal must be something you can experience yourself.

Establishing long-term goals then enables you to set intermediate goals and shorter range objectives. Objectives determine the conditions, resources, and knowledge that you need in order to achieve your goals.

Objectives should be prioritized according to how much they contribute to your goals. If an objective or an activity does not work to achieve your goals, change or replace that objective so that it does. To increase the chance of success, you need to be flexible.

"More men fail through lack of purpose than lack of talent."

BILL SUNDAY

Following is an example of a **long-term goal** and related **intermediate goals,** and **short** term **objectives**:

Long-Term Goal:	- Career as a Counselor/Psychologist (6 to 8 years).
Intermediate Goals:	- Enter a Ph.D. or Master's program in Counseling or Clinical Psychology (3 to 5 years). - Graduate Assistantship or Counseling job at the Bachelor's level (2 to 4 years).
Short-Term Objectives:	- Major in psychology. - Courses in education, biology, and statistics. - Volunteer work as a hot-line counselor. - Volunteer or paid work as a research assistant (to generate reference letters from faculty). - Study skills course to improve grades and study habits.

Complete Activity # 3
Goal Setting

ACTIVITY 3: GOAL SETTING

"When we align our daily choices with what matters most, we significantly increase our productivity and sense of purpose."

Stephen Covey

Identify your long-term goal(s), intermediate goals and short-term objectives. For long-term and intermediate goals, indicate how long (number of years) you anticipate it will take to achieve your goals.

Long-term Goal(s)	
Intermediate Goals	
Short-term Objectives	

Now update your Learning Journal (page 53)

"

*Watches are so named as a reminder -
if you don't watch carefully what you do with
your time, it will slip away from you.*

DREW SIRTORS

"

THE TIME MATRIX

For most people, the majority of tasks faced during a day seem equally urgent and important. However, many of the urgent activities we become involved in are not really important in the long run.

The judgement as to whether activities are urgent, important, both, or neither, is crucial to effective time management. Urgent tasks have short-term consequences while important tasks are those with long-term goal-related implications.

	Urgent	Not Urgent
Important	**Quadrant 1 MANAGE** • Crisis • Medical emergencies • Pressing problems • Deadline-driven projects • Last-minute preparations for scheduled activities	**Quadrant 2 FOCUS** • Preparation/planning • Prevention • Values clarification • Exercise • Relationship-building • True recreation/relaxation
Not Important	**Quadrant 3 AVOID** • Interruptions, some calls • Some mail, email and reports • Some meetings • Many "pressing" matters • Many popular activities	**Quadrant 4 AVOID** • Trivia, busywork • Junk mail • Some phone messages/email • Time wasters • Escape activities • Viewing mindless TV shows

Stephen Covey's Time Management Matrix

Those who are poor at time management tend to spend most of their time in quadrants 1 and 3. These people tend to prioritize their tasks and consequently their time, according to who shouted last and loudest. Any spare time is typically spent in quadrant 4, which comprises only of aimless and non-productive activities. Most people spend the least amount of time in quadrant 2, which is the most critical for success.

"The greatest value of the planning process is not what it does to your schedule, but what it does to your head. As you begin to think more in terms of importance, you begin to see time differently. You become empowered to put first things first in your life in a significant way."

STEPHEN COVEY

Complete Activity # 4
The Time Matrix

ACTIVITY 4: THE TIME MATRIX

Identify the important and non-important, and urgent and non-urgent tasks that you currently face in your day-to-day activities.

	Urgent	Not Urgent
Important	Quadrant 1	Quadrant 2
Not Important	Quadrant 3	Quadrant 4

ACTIVITY 4: CONTINUED

Identify some actions that you could take immediately to improve time management effectiveness.

I could manage my tasks in Quadrant 1 by…	
I could spend more time in Quadrant 2 by…	
I could spend less time in Quadrant 3 and Quadrant 4 by…	

Now update your Learning Journal (page 53)

"

"The Future is something which everyone reaches at the rate of sixty minutes an hour, whatever he does, whoever he is."

C.S. LEWIS

"

PART 3
DAILY AND WEEKLY ACTIONS

PLANNING & PRIORITIZING

"Planning and prioritizing is the answer to time management problems - not computers, efficiency experts, or matrix scheduling. You do not need to do work faster or to eliminate gaps in productivity to make better use of your time. You need to spend more time on the right things..."

C. RAY JOHNSON

The heart of effective time management is in weekly and daily planning. Using time to think and plan is time well-spent. If you fail to take time for planning, you are, in effect, planning to fail.

One key reason why planning and prioritizing works, is the 80/20 Rule. The 80/20 Rule states that 80 percent of our typical activities contribute less than 20 percent to the value of our work. So, if you do only the most important 20 percent of your tasks you still get most of the value.

Planning is preparing a sequence of action steps to achieve specific objectives, reducing the necessary time and effort required to accomplish a goal. Planning allows you to clearly measure progress towards your goals, and make appropriate decisions on where to direct your energies.

Failure to plan and prioritize effectively makes it difficult to motivate yourself to complete important tasks in your schedule that are not immediately gratifying. It also allows others to interrupt and manipulate your schedule, staking their claim on your time.

If you are subject to demand and request by others in your organization, you need to recondition their expectations as to your availability. Produce a daily or weekly schedule, showing your planned activities and time-slots for everything that you do. This is a vital tool in helping you to justify to others why you can schedule their demands only when it suits you, not them.

Complete Activity # 5
My Biological Prime Time

ACTIVITY 5: MY BIOLOGICAL PRIME TIME

Plot your personal work performance and energy levels throughout the course of the day.

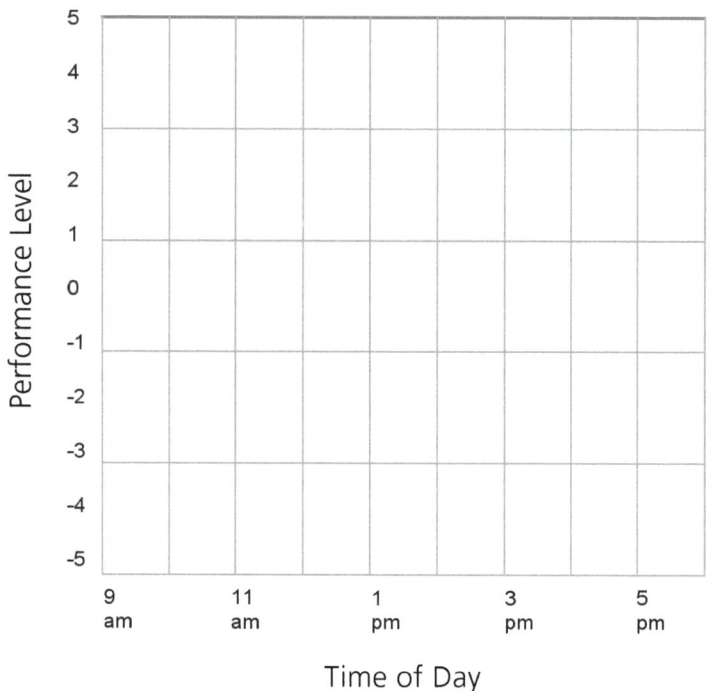

The best time for my A priorities is _____

The best time for my B priorities is _____

The best time for my C priorities is _____

Now update your Learning Journal (page 53)

THE DAILY TO DO LIST

Use a simple daily list or weekly planner to manage and guard your planned activities. Effective time management is about scheduling activities into time slots and then protecting those activities from interruptions, whether from other people or from your own distractions.

Prioritize your planned activities according to how relevant they are in achieving your short-term objectives and long-term goals. Priorities are determined by identifying both urgent and important tasks and assigning a simple ABC rating.

A = **Highest Priority**
(urgent and important tasks)

B = **Moderate Priority**
(urgent or important - these account for most of your work)

C = **Lowest Priority**
(not urgent or important but do need to be completed when time allows)

Following is a 'priorities flowchart' to help you clearly identify A, B & C tasks.

"Never let yesterday use up today."

RICHARD H. NELSON

The daily To Do list is simply a list of tasks that you need to accomplish in a day. In order to create an effective daily list you need to know what your activities and obligations are for several weeks, then prioritize accordingly. Following is an sample daily To Do List incorporating the A-B-C priority system. This a schedule for David, a student who works and attends law school.

Daily To Do List

Status	Priority ABC	Task
	A	Review notes for legal ethics class
	C	Study for contracts class
	B	Work out at the gym
	A	Discuss Sam's school results
	A	Prepare client brief for tomorrow
	C	Write an email to sister
	A	Do contracts assignment
	C	Review notes for test next week
	A	Arrange playdate with Toni
	B	Library research
	C	Football Club Meeting

In this schedule it is possible to identify some of David's long-term goals - to finish law school, and to be a good husband and father. This schedule is quite balanced as it also includes time for exercise and family contact.

Complete Activity # 6
The Daily To Do List

ACTIVITY 6: THE DAILY TO DO LIST

 Download the TPC Daily To Do List from https://www.catherinemattiske.com/books

Activity using the TPC Daily To Do List

Download and complete the Daily To Do List for your next work day. Be sure to allocate A, B or C priorities according to how well these tasks and activities contribute to the achievement of your goals.

Now update your Learning Journal (page 53)

THE WEEKLY PLANNER

A weekly planner allows you to allocate time, hour-by-hour throughout the course of the day and the week, giving you very clear guidelines around what to do and when to do it. Although some people may find this confining, others welcome the order and control that this system provides.

The key to a successful weekly plan is to keep to the schedule, be realistic about what you can achieve, allow plenty of free time for recreation, and keep your longer term goals and priorities in mind.

Following is a sample Weekly Planner. Again, this is a schedule for David, who works and attends law school. One of David's days have been completed as a an example.

Weekly Planner

Week Beginning: July 3 • **Week Ending:** July 9
Weekly Goal: Prepare for upcoming law exams and spend quality time with family

	MON	TUES	WED	THURS	FRI
Today's Priorities	Client brief for tomorrow and complete contracts assignment				
Appointments / Commitments					
6am	Gym				
7am	Breakfast				
8am	Plan daily to do list, check email				
9am	Appraisal meeting with manager				
10am	Client meeting				
11am	Prepare client brief for tomorrow				
12noon	Lunch				
1pm	Return phone calls/ emails				
2pm	Thinking time for new project				
3pm	Law library – case research				
4pm	Complete contracts assignment				
5pm	Home				
6pm	Arrange playdate with Toni				
7pm	Discuss Sam's school results				
8pm	Write email to sister				
Evening					

© 2022, TPC - The Performance Company Pty Limited. All rights reserved.

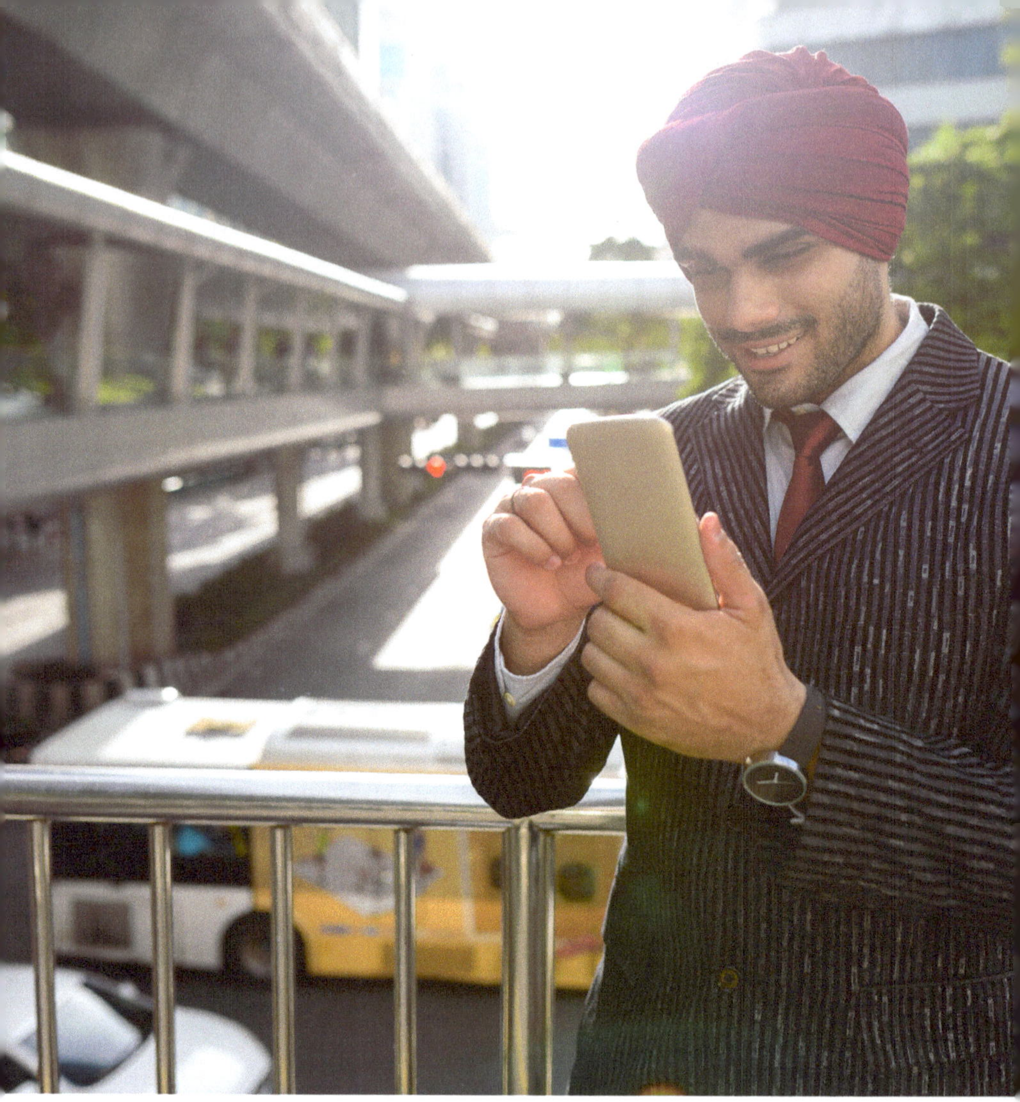

Complete Activity # 7
The Weekly Planner

ACTIVITY 7: THE WEEKLY PLANNER

 Download the TPC Weekly Planner from https://www.catherinemattiske.com/books

Activity using the TPC Weekly Planner

Download and complete the Weekly Planner for next week. Again, when scheduling tasks or activities think about how well these contribute to the achievement of your goals.

Now update your Learning Journal (page 53)

> "If you want work well done, select a busy man - the other kind has no time."
>
> ELBERT HUBBARD

TIPS AND TRAPS

PART 4

MANAGING UNPLANNED TASKS & INTERRUPTIONS

Despite your best efforts to manage time effectively, you will always encounter unplanned tasks and interruptions to your schedule. These will be easier to manage by adopting the 4 D's technique.

The 4 D's

Do It - This means perform the necessary task(s) contained in the letter, email, phone call or memo. Once you have completed these tasks, any work or correspondence should be filed, re-routed to someone else or discarded. Make sure that doing the task won't interfere with your daily schedule an put other tasks off track.

Drop It - This means that further action needs to be taken on this task, but not right now, so you drop it into a file. It may be a good idea to file it in an electronic or physical "reminder file". Make sure you add the task to your master task list, give it a due date, and prioritize it.

Delegate It - This means that you immediately give this task to someone else, whether this person is someone in your company, a client, a vendor, or someone else that you outsource to. Not everything that ends up on your desk needs to be done by you.

Dump It - This is the greatest one of them all. It is probably safe to say that a huge percentage of the paper that enters your office or e-mails that you receive can be immediately discarded.

It is also important to allow time for interruptions and distractions. Time management experts often suggest planning for just 50 percent or less of one's time. With only 50 percent of your time planned, you will have the flexibility to handle interruptions and the unplanned "emergency."

When you expect to be interrupted, schedule routine tasks. Save larger blocks of time for your priorities. When interrupted, ask Alan Lakein's crucial question, "What is the most important thing I can be doing with my time right now?" to help you get back on track fast.

Where possible, be absolutely firm in dealing with time allocated for meetings, paperwork, emails, telephone calls and visitors. If you can't stop interruptions then go elsewhere when you need time alone. Fight for your right to work uninterrupted when you need to.

 **Complete Activity # 8**
Managing Interruptions

ACTIVITY 8: MANAGING INTERRUPTIONS

Identify the time management issues in the following picture.

The issues in this picture are:

_____
_____
_____
_____
_____
_____

_____
_____

Identify the time management issues in the following picture regarding interruptions:

The issues in this picture are:

_____
_____
_____
_____
_____
_____
_____

_____

ACTIVITY 8: CONTINUED

Think about strategies to reduce your level of interruptions.

I can reduce my level of interruptions by…

Now update your Learning Journal (page 53)

CLEARING THE CLUTTER

Effective time management is also about reviewing your work environment, office layout, IT equipment etc, and setting it up for efficiency. Efficient organization of your physical and digital work space can make an enormous difference to your productivity. Regularly tidy up your work area and keep paperwork filed away unless you are working on it. Keep a clean desk and computer desktop, and well organized filing systems, without becoming obsessive.

"There's never enough time to do all the nothing you want."

BILL WATTERSON

Tips for organizing your workspace

- Keep work surfaces as clear as possible at all times.
- Tidy desk drawers, and keep them ordered.
- Keep pens, pencils, tape, glue, rulers etc together in a single, accessible container.
- Keep your desk clear of everything but the job in hand.
- In the same way, tidy and clear your computer desktop, device screens and electronic files and apps

Tips for filing - electronic and hard copy files

- Set up a filing system that will grow with you.
- Go through your files regularly and discard files/documents that you no longer need.
- Use a coding system that allows you to locate files quickly at a glance. This reduces the time you spend searching for documents, increasing the efficiency of your work practices.
- Subdivide files into smaller files to make them more manageable and easy to identify.
- File only essential documents/items that will be used for future reference.
- Set aside time for filing and organization – either at the end of every day or the end of every week.

"There is more to life than increasing speed."

MOHANDAS K GANDHI

TIME MANAGEMENT QUICK TIPS

> "The bad news is that time flies. The good news is that you're the pilot."
>
> MICHAEL ALTSCHULER

1. If you are a slave to your email system or other applications, turn off the notifications. Establish a new habit of checking your messages at regular intervals that don't disturb your focus time.

2. When you are faced with a pile of things to do, go through them quickly and make a list of what needs to be done and when. After this, handle each item only once. Do not under any circumstances pick up a job, do a bit of it, then put it back on the pile. Do not start lots of jobs at the same time.

3. Delegate as much as possible to others. Good delegation saves you time, and can develop and motivate others around you.

4. Learn to say 'No', politely and constructively. Don't make a rod for your own back. Be careful about accepting sideways delegation from your peers. If you find it difficult to say 'no' you'll find it easier by using business reasons to justify your position. Show others your schedule to prove how you prioritize and manage your time for the good of the business.

5. Always probe deadlines to establish the true situation - those asking you to do things will often say 'now' when 'later today' or 'by the end of the week' would be perfectly acceptable. Appeal to the other person's own sense of time management.

6. Conquer procrastination on big tasks by never trying to 'eat an elephant

all in one go'. Break down big tasks into digestible chunks. One technique is to try the "swiss cheese" method prescribed by Alan Lakein. When you are avoiding something, break it into smaller tasks, or allocate small amounts of time to work on the big task. By doing a little at a time you will eventually reach a point where the end is in sight and you want to finish.

7. Avoid being a perfectionist. While some things need to be closer to perfect than others, paying unnecessary attention to detail can be a form of procrastination.

"Half our life is spent trying to find something to do with the time we have rushed through life trying to save."

WILL ROGERS

8. Review all of the regular reports that you write and receive for usefulness, and make or recommend changes. Set up an acceptable template for the regular weekly or monthly reports, so that you only need to slot in updated figures and narrative each time. Where possible, don't reinvent the wheel.

9. Challenge any task that could be wasting time and effort, particularly habitual tasks, meetings and reports where responsibility is inherited. Don't just assume that because something has always been done, that it is appropriate or even required.

10. Reward yourself. Even for small successes, celebrate achievement of goals. Promise yourself a reward for completing each task, or finishing the total job. Then keep your promise to yourself and indulge in your reward. Doing so will help you maintain the necessary balance in life between work and play.

Complete Activity # 9
Time Management Quick Tips

ACTIVITY 9: TIME MANAGEMENT QUICK TIPS

Select your top 3 quick tips and state how you will implement these back in the workplace.

My top 3 quick tips are…	I will implement this tip by….
1.	
2.	
3.	

Now update your Learning Journal (page 53)

"There is one kind of robber whom the law does not strike at, and who steals what is most precious to men: time."

NAPOLEON I, MAXIMS, 1815

A FINAL THOUGHT

PART 5

ONE GRAIN AT A TIME...

"The inertia hardest to overcome is that of perfectly good seconds."

MARTIN H. FISCHER

Most of us think of ourselves as standing wearily and helplessly at the centre of a circle, bristling with tasks, burdens, problems, annoyances and responsibilities, which are rushing upon us.

At every moment we have a dozen different things to do, a dozen problems to solve, a dozen strains to endure. We see ourselves as over driven, overburdened, overtired. This is a common mental picture - and it is totally false. No one of us, however crowded his life, has such an existence.

What is the true picture of your life? Imagine that there is an hourglass on your desk. Connecting the bowl at the top with the bowl at the bottom is a tub so thin that only one grain of sand can pass through at a time.

That is the true picture of your life, even on a super busy day. The crowded hours come to you always one moment at a time. That is the only way they can come. The day may bring many tasks, many problems, many strains, but invariably they come in single file.

You want to gain emotional poise? Remember the hourglass, the grains of sand dropping one by one.

James Gordon Gilkey

"Don't say you don't have enough time. You have exactly the same number of hours per day that were given to Helen Keller, Pasteur, Michelangelo, Mother Teresa, Leonardo da Vinci, Thomas Jefferson, and Albert Einstein."

H. JACKSON BROWN

> *Time is the coin of your life.*
> *It is the only coin you have, and only*
> *you can determine how it will be spent.*
> *Be careful lest you let other people*
> *spend it for you.*
>
> CARL SANDBERG

Section 2
LEARNING JOURNAL

The Learning Journal is used throughout the process to record your key learnings, hot tips and things to remember.

Update your Learning Journal at anytime. Ensure you complete your Learning Journal after you finish each activity. Then turn back to the Learning Short-take® to continue your learning.

LEARNING JOURNAL

As you work through this Learning Short-take®, make detailed notes on this page of the lessons you have learned and any useful skill areas. For each lesson or refresher point think about how you could further develop this skill. Your coach will want to discuss these with you in your Skill Development Action Planning meeting.

"…that is what learning is.
You suddenly understand something you've understood all your life, but in a new way."

DORIS LESSING

"Act as though it were impossible to fail."

WINSTON CHURCHILL

"The wise do at once what the fool does later."
BALTASAR GRACIAN (1601-58), SPANISH JESUIT PRIEST AND AUTHOR.

Learning or Idea	Action to be taken	Result Expected

Learning Journal - continued

Learning or Idea	Action to be taken	Result Expected

> *"Anyone who stops learning is old, whether at twenty or eighty."*
>
> HENRY FORD

Learning or Idea	Action to be taken	Result Expected

"

*It's a strange thing, but when you
are dreading something, and would
give anything to slow down time,
it has a disobliging habit of speeding up.*

J.K. ROWLING

"

Section 3

SKILL DEVELOPMENT ACTION PLAN

Your Skill Development Action Plan is the last Step in the process. After you have completed the Learning Short-take® and all Activities, update your Learning Journal, then complete this section.

SKILL DEVELOPMENT ACTION PLAN

This is the most important part of the program - your individual Skill Development Action Plan.

You need to complete this plan before meeting with your manager or prior to on-going coaching. You will discuss it in detail with your manager or coach as he or she will ensure that you have everything you need to complete the tasks and activities.

Once you have completed your **Skill Development Action Plan** schedule a meeting time with your manager or coach to review your plan. Take your Learning Short-take® and all other documentation received during the training course to this meeting.

Remember - you have committed to your **Skill Development Action Plan**, and need to make time to complete your tasks!

"The mind, once stretched by a new idea, never regains its original dimensions."

OLIVER WENDELL HOLMES

"Whatever you can do or dream you can - begin it. Boldness has genius, power and magic."

JOHANN WOLFGANG VON GOETHE

> *"Imagination is the eye of the soul."*
> JOSEPH JOUBERT (1754-1824)

Task or activity (Be specific)	Measure (this will help you to know you have achieved it)	Date (Be specific)
Reflect on your Learning Journal. Transfer action items that you can apply to your job. Ensure that you include some 'stretch goals' and also a blend of short, medium and long term goals.	Apart from you, who else is needed to assist you in achieving your goal.	Be specific. A general date such as 'Quarter 1', 'August', or 'by end of year' is vague and more likely to result in not achieving your target. Be specific – e.g. 22nd November.

IDEAS FOR DISCUSSION WITH MY MANAGER

Ideas

CONGRATULATIONS!

You've now completed this Learning Short-take®.

Meet with your Manager/Coach to discuss your
Skill Development Action Plan.

"

For disappearing acts, it's hard to beat what happens to the eight hours supposedly left after eight of sleep and eight of work.

DOUG LARSON

"

Overview

Time is our most unique and valuable resource. It is the one thing that we all have in common: we all have 24 hours in a day and 168 hours in a week. We cannot slow time down, stop time, or negotiate with time. Time is irretrievable and once wasted it is gone forever. Control and discipline are required to make the most of every minute.

Quick Reference

> *The reason most people never reach their goals is that they don't define them, or ever seriously consider them as believable or achievable.*
>
> — DENIS WATLEY

SMART Goal Setting

Specific - Your goal must be specific.

Measurable - You must be able to measure progress towards your goal.

Attainable - Your goal must be something that you can actually attain.

Realistic - Your goal must be realistic, given who you are.

Tangible - Your goal must be something you can experience yourself.

Quick Reference

The Time Matrix

	Urgent	Not Urgent
Important	**Quadrant 1 MANAGE** - Crisis - Medical emergencies - Pressing problems - Deadline-driven projects - Last-minute preparations for scheduled activities	**Quadrant 2 FOCUS** - Preparation/planning - Prevention - Values clarification - Exercise - Relationship-building - True recreation/relaxation
Not Important	**Quadrant 3 AVOID** - Interruptions, some calls - Some mail, email and reports - Some meetings - Many "pressing" matters - Many popular activities	**Quadrant 4 AVOID** - Trivia, busywork - Junk mail - Some phone messages/email - Time wasters - Escape activities - Viewing mindless TV shows

© 2022, TPC - The Performance Company Pty Limited. All rights reserved.

"

The greatest value of the planning process is not what it does to your schedule, but what it does to your head. As you begin to think more in terms of importance, you begin to see time differently. You become empowered to put first things first in your life in a significant way.

STEPHEN COVEY

"

Quick Reference

Planning & Prioritizing

The heart of effective time management is in weekly and daily planning. Using time to think and plan is time well-spent. If you fail to take time for planning, you are, in effect, planning to fail.

"

Planning and prioritizing is the answer to time management problems - not computers, efficiency experts, or matrix scheduling. You do not need to do work faster or to eliminate gaps in productivity to make better use of your time. You need to spend more time on the right things...

C. RAY JOHNSON

"

Quick Reference

Daily or Weekly Schedules

If you are subject to demand and request by others in your organization, you need to recondition their expectations as to your availability. Produce a daily or weekly schedule, showing your planned activities and time-slots for everything that you do. This is a vital tool in helping you to justify to others why you can schedule their demands only when it suits you, not them.

A, B, C Priorities

Prioritize your planned activities according to how relevant they are in achieving your short-term objectives and long-term goals. Priorities are determined by identifying both urgent and important tasks and assigning a simple ABC rating.

A = Highest Priority (urgent and important tasks)

B = Moderate Priority (urgent or important - these account for most of your work)

C = Lowest Priority (not urgent or important but do need to be completed when time allows)

Quick Reference

Don't say you don't have enough time. You have exactly the same number of hours per day that were given to Helen Keller, Pasteur, Michelangelo, Mother Teresa, Leonardo da Vinci, Thomas Jefferson, and Albert Einstein.

H. JACKSON BROWN

Managing Unplanned Tasks & Interruptions - The 4 D's

Do It - This means perform the necessary task(s) contained in the letter, email, phone call or memo.

Drop It - This means that further action needs to be taken on this task, but not right now, so you drop it into a physical or electronic file.

Delegate It - This means that you immediately give this task to someone else, whether this person is someone in your company, a client, a vendor, or someone else that you outsource to.

Dump It - This is the greatest one of them all. It is probably safe to say that a huge percentage of the paper that enters your office or e-mails that you receive can be immediately discarded.

Quick Reference

*The bad news is that time flies.
The good news is that you're the pilot.*

MICHAEL ALTSCHULER

NEXT STEPS

Congratulations! You have now completed this Learning Short-take® title. The entire list of Learning Short-takes® can be found on the catherinemattiske.com website.

In this section we have suggested Learning Short-take® titles for you that will build your learning. You may order these Learning Short-takes® online at https://www.catherinemattiske.com/books or from your bookstores.

Creative Business Thinking
Developing the Skills for Thinking Outside the Box

Learning Short-take® Outline

Creative Business Thinking includes a library of brilliant creativity tools, fun activities, and challenging business scenarios. These will help to stretch your thinking by deliberately challenging existing perspectives and considering alternative ways of working.

Creative Business Thinking is packed with techniques for creative thinking and fun 'mind quiz' activities. **Creative Business Thinking** constructively challenges the status quo to enable new ideas to surface and solve problems in ways that may not initially come to mind.

Within each of us there exists an infinite capacity for creating ideas and nurturing them through to innovation. **Creative Business Thinking** emphasizes pragmatic tools and techniques to successfully unlock creative potential.

Creative Business Thinking includes the job aid **15 Creativity Techniques for Problem Solving**, and the **Creative Business Thinking Techniques Wall Chart**, provided to you as free downloadable tools.

Learning Objectives

- Undertake a self assessment in creativity.
- List personal and organizational creative contributions.
- Choose personal creative techniques to be used in the workplace.
- Match group creativity techniques with case study applications.
- Use six thinking hats to solve a business challenge.
- Create a plan for an upcoming team meeting employing creative thinking techniques.

Course Content

- Part 1: Creativity and lateral thinking
- Part 2: Unleash those creative forces
- Part 3: Personal creative thinking techniques
- Part 4: Tools for Creative Business Thinking
  - 6 thinking hats
  - Brainstorming
  - Metaphors
  - Cause & effect (Fishbone Diagram)
  - Work breakdown structure
  - 5-Why's
  - Different point of view
  - Concept mapping / Mind mapping
- Part 5: Answers

Making Meetings Work
Getting the Most out of Meetings

Learning Short-take® Outline

Making Meetings Work combines self-study with realistic workplace activities to provide you with the key skills and techniques to make meetings work. Your meetings will become more focused, efficient, targeted and more likely to have a productive impact on the company's bottom-line. You will learn how to more effectively prepare, manage, facilitate and actively participate in meetings.

It is estimated that the average professional spends 61.5 hours per month in meetings, or two weeks every year. It is also estimated that at least 50% of this time is wasted in unproductive meeting activity. **Making Meetings Work** will provide you with the tools to help you save time and money.

Making Meetings Work includes the **Meeting Administration Checklist**, **Meeting Agenda** and **Meeting Minutes** provided as free downloadable tools.

Course Content

- Part 1: Types of Meetings
- Part 2: Why Meetings Fail
- Part 3: Solutions to Meeting Barriers
- Part 4: Planning the Meeting
- Part 5: Preparing the Agenda
- Part 6: Conducting the Meeting

Learning Objectives

- Evaluate your current level of meeting success.
- Identify the various types of meetings and explain key differences.
- Develop solutions to common meeting problems.
- Outline the steps for a successful meeting.
- Carry out meeting planning and preparation.
- Create a Skill Development Action Plan.

Listen and Be Listened To
Transform communication in a world of distraction

Learning Short-take® Outline

combines self-study with realistic workplace activities to provide you with the key skills and techniques of effective and enhanced listening. You will learn to build more effective work relationships with your co-workers and leaders by tuning into key communication messages and responding appropriately. You will learn tips, tricks and techniques to boost active listening capability and discover that effective listening helps command respect from both the speakers and listeners point of view.

Our unique view of the world and personal style - based on our values, beliefs, attitudes and behaviors - affects how we act, perceive information, and communicate with others. It also influences the way we listen and how others listen to us. When we expect to hear certain things, we may pay attention to only what interests us. Our perception about a person, situation or subject influences our reception of information, and how much attention we choose to pay. **Listen and Be Listened To** breaks down the art and skill of active listening which is critical to building and maintaining effective working relationships.

Listen and Be Listened To includes an impactful 'Listening Tips' Wall Chart, provided to you as a free download.

Learning Objectives

- Define listening.
- Explain why listening is important.
- Identify the barriers to effective listening.
- Identify their listening style and the listening style of others.
- Demonstrate techniques for active listening.
- Create a Skill Development Action Plan.

Course Content

- Part 1: Listening & Communication
- Part 2: Listening versus Hearing
- Part 3: Barriers to Effective Listening
- Part 4: Your Natural Listening Style
- Part 5: Passive Listening
- Part 6: Active Listening
- Part 7: Better Questions, Better Answers

www.catherinemattiske.com

www.ingramcontent.com/pod-product-compliance
Lightning Source LLC
Chambersburg PA
CBHW041549110526
R18277000001B/R182770PG44587CBX00001B/1